Uplifting and Encouraging Caregivers

Johnnita Robinson

Uplifting and Encouraging Caregivers

Copyright © 2016 JOHNNITA ROBINSON

Cover page designed by Styles Print.

ISBN:0692673792
ISBN-13:9780692673799

DEDICATION

This book is for every Caregiver who may not have been noticed for what they have done or for what they do. You should know that your labor of love is not in vain. It takes someone very special to be a Caregiver. It takes someone who is neither selfish nor self-centered to take on the responsibility of caring for another human being regardless of the length of time. You truly are special, loving and more valuable than you will ever know!

Johnnita L Robinson

CONTENTS

ACKNOWLEDGEMENTS

To my Heavenly, Loving, Caring Father, thank you for planting the desire in me to write this book. You have stuck by me when others have left me. You have made me feel like I could do any and everything! It's because of the revelation of your Word that has caused me to think BIGGER! THE BEST IS YET TO COME!!

To my sister Delisa who has been a joy to care for. She has been and still is my best friend. She encouraged me when I was a single mother, as well as with recently earning my Degree. Even though she was dealing with her own diagnosis, she always found ways to uplift me. As we are standing on the Word of God for the manifestation of her healing together, she never ceases to amaze me with her positive outlook on life. Our parents would be so proud of the way that we have looked out for one another!

To my son Jeremiah Robinson, thank you for your help during the beginning years.

To my cousins James & Carmen Byars, thank you for all that you have done during that time in my life and all that you still continue to do. You will never know how much you have blessed me!!

To my grandchildren, Jordan and Jayda, Nana is thankful to have you as her grandbabies. I pray that as you grow up, you will be thankful to have me as well.

To the church members of Fountain of Faith Christian Center who have assisted me in some kind of way, I thank you dearly! It is so wonderful to be a part of such a loving church.

To my other family members who have always been there as well have been there over the years. Thank you from the bottom of my heart!

To Mr. & Mrs. Walter Gardner, you truly have been a blessing in so many ways that you have no idea. Thank you!

To Erica Thompson, thank you for your complimentary and encouraging words, and for never charging Delisa for getting her hair done during the first year of her diagnosis. You will never be forgotten.

To my Uncle James E. Byars, Sr, you are awesome! Anytime we called, you were always there!

Foreword

It takes a special person to care for someone consistently for the past 10 years while working full time, going to school part time, working part time at church, and coming home to another full time job to take care of her sister. I have watched Johnnita do this for the last several years, with a great attitude and a true love for her sister! It has made her job a lot better than what it could have been with God in her life! This is a must read for those in similar situations. With God's help, you can truly do all things through Christ! Philippians 4:13

Pastor James E Byars, Jr.

Fountain of Faith Christian Center, Louisville, KY

FOREWORD

"A Caregivers Perspective" has been written by my cousin and good friend Johnnita Robinson. During an unthinkable day in 2007, she was immediately thrust into a caregiver mode. It was not easy receiving the news of her sister's diagnosis, but she never gave caring for her sister a second thought. She immediately took on the responsibility of caring for her adult sister with what seems like with ease. Her patience, love, energy and caring attitude is beyond our families' comprehension. Although, it can be obviously challenging at times, she seems to handle her extra responsibilities very well.

As you read this book, you will gain practical insight into caring for a loved one at home. As she shares her experience, trust that she has walked out every step and will share what worked well and what did not work so well. As the saying goes, "Why re-invent the wheel?" Any caregiver who listens to and applies what she shares can glean from her experience.

Minister Carmen Byars

Fountain of Faith Christian Center, Louisville, KY

JOHNNITA ROBINSON

Introduction

This book was written to assist Caregivers with everything that they need to be better Caregivers. So often Caregivers are always taking care of others and fall short in taking care of themselves. This book will uplift you and encourage you as well as motivate you to take better care of YOU!

When I became a Caregiver, there was little information available on being a Caregiver. I decided to become an instrument to help other Caregivers in any way that I could. This book is all about YOU Caregiver.

It will show you how important it is in making sure you are living your life while you are caring for someone else and the importance of moving forward, no matter what has happened in your life.

More importantly, it will help you not to give up, regardless of what comes your way. If you do not take care of yourself, then you will not be able to take care of anyone else. It can be overwhelming at times when you are taking care of others, which is why it is very important to take care of YOU!

CHAPTER 1

My Personal Story

To all the Caregivers, please hear me when I say I understand what you are going through. Our situations or the level of the person that we are caring for may be different. But nevertheless, we are Caregivers.

It started for me as a Caregiver in 2007. My sister was diagnosed with an autoimmune disease in 2005, but was still able to function on her own. She was living alone at the time, and was able to take care of her own needs. But because of the symptoms, such as pain in the legs, arms as well as her eyesight dimming, she had to move in with me because she could no longer take care of herself. She had lost her job, so there was no way for her to support herself financially.

She moved in with me in 2005 and pretty much was able to still cook and clean as well as bathe herself. I know it was very hard for her to grasp, but we knew it had to be done. Just think, all of your adult life how hard it would be for you to go from being independent to being dependent on another person. My heart ached for her. And there were plenty of times I would just cry, because I knew that things were changing for her that we all did not expect or anticipate.

After a period of time, things started to get physically worse for her in 2007. She started waking up in the middle of the night to urinating frequently. I would hear her running to the bathroom nightly just to try and make it before any accidents occurred. With this happening, it would cause my son and me to have to get up at night as well. The pain in her legs and her spine began to worsen. Because of the pain she was having in her spine, it was causing her to bend over. But I have to say, she kept pushing herself. I would come home from work and see where she had done everything she could to keep herself from giving up.

She would have the house thoroughly cleaned, meals cooked and clothes as well as dishes washed, dried and placed where they belonged. It was not asked of her. It was something she felt like she needed to do to keep her sanity. This was a woman who had worked since she was fourteen, up until this diagnosis came upon her. So I understood why she could not just sit still at home and do nothing. She had always been a person that paid her own bills, did her own grocery shopping and purchased her own clothing whenever she needed. And if there was anything else that needed to be done, she would do it.

And from that point on, I had to take her to the hospital, because of so many changes that were taking place in her body. It seemed as if we lived at the hospital for months at a time.

The Autoimmune disease had basically attacked her nerves and her immune system. And because of the attack, the entire right side of her body was affected. It caused her right hand to close, and not be of use. It also caused her right leg to become weaker than her left leg, which was her stronger side to begin with.

I felt as if I was in a bad dream and could not wake

up. I am her only sister and she also has two brothers. But
they had no idea of what I had to endure. I learned a lot
during that time. I am not sexist, but women are a lot
stronger than men. Maybe not physically, but mentally in a
lot of ways. God made us that way and I began to see why. I
had so many decisions to make and I did not know where to
begin. During 2007, as I stated earlier, is when all the
changes began to take place. I had taken her to the hospital it
seemed liked for the twentieth time.

During these times, she had no idea mentally what
was going on. I had to keep praying for her and with her no
matter what I saw, and regardless of what the doctors were
saying. The last time that she was in the hospital, the doctors
suggested that she needed to be somewhere where she could
be cared for 24 hours a day for a while.

I had a relative who worked in a nursing
home/rehabilitation facility. She suggested that I take her
there until she became well enough to be home again. That
was not an easy suggestion to take. I had to pray about it,
because I had heard of the horror stories that took place in

that type of environment. Also, I did not want her to be out of my sight. My sister and I have been close since we were little girls. I am only 11 months older than her. We had always talked just about everything. We would have our sister spats when we were younger as sisters do. But we would always look out for one another. She was the maid of honor in my wedding and she was my son's second mom.

We lost our parents when I was twenty two and she was twenty one. So we always had each other to lean on at all times. A sister's bond is unbreakable and priceless. So the thought of placing her in a nursing home was far from what I wanted to do. But I really did not have a choice. I worked full time and I had a son that was still in high school. So there was no one to look after her.

The decision was finally made. In June 2007, she was taken from the hospital to the nursing home. It was one of the biggest and hardest decisions I had ever made. Her doctors had given up on her and really did not think she would live long. They would not say it flat out right, but they would say that there was nothing else that they could do for her.

She was at the nursing home for a year. And I have to tell you, I was there more than I was at home. It broke my heart to leave her there at night. I had struggled to leave her with no family around. It was more work for me to have her there than to keep her at home. I had to make sure that they were giving her the correct medications and I had to make sure she was receiving physical and occupational therapy at all times.

You see, I had heard of so many unfortunate stories about nursing homes, such as patients not being taking care of properly, patients not being bathed consistently, patient's clothes being misplaced or stolen out of their rooms. Even worse, the wrong dosage of medicines being given to the patients. I just could not take a chance on anything detrimental happening to her. Even though she was an adult, I felt like her mother in a sense. Being that our parents had passed away years ago, and by my being the oldest, I felt like it was my place to take care of her. Needless to say, that was a very challenging year.

In the very beginning I had to sign all of these papers giving them permission to do whatever they needed to do to assist her.

She had just begun receiving her social security disability. The nursing home took all of that except forty dollars. Since she was now living there and the facility had to be paid for, it had to come out of her finances.

And then I thought what next. It was like taking care of two homes at one time. She would need personal items and more clothing that fitted properly. She was picking up weight, because of not being physically active. So clothing was always being purchased, in order for her to be comfortable.

At that time I had family members as well as church members come and sit with her, which was a huge blessing to me. I did not have to be there seven days a week like I did in the beginning. But I would always come at unexpected times to be with her as well as check on the staff. I enjoyed coming early in the morning before I went to work. Whether it was just to read scriptures, pray or just listen to her. A lot of times she did not know what was going on.

An Autoimmune disease not only affects the neurological system, but it can affect the brain as well as other organs of the body. Even to this day, she does not remember a lot about being there. I must admit that it was not all bad. But there was one of few instances when she was there where they had called me stating that she was not talking at all. And I thought to myself, that is not like her.

After work, I had gone to check on her. And it was true. She was not talking at all. She would not utter a word, and she would just stare into space. The nurse had listened to her lungs and thought she needed to go to the hospital. Well, come to find out she had pneumonia in one of her lungs. I looked somewhat stunned and thought how did she get that? She had never had it before. But she did somehow contract it. She had to stay in the hospital for a couple of days.

After numerous days of receiving antibiotics and lots of prayers, she began to speak and became so much better. She was released and was able to go back to the nursing facility. They were very helpful in taking care of her when she returned. For the most part, anything they could do to assist her, they did.

There were some good people that assisted her. However, I just would not want to do it again. I would not wish it on any one to have to deal with taking care of someone that needed the type of assistance that she did. It not only breaks you down physically, but it can break you down mentally.

I have compassion for people that have to stay in those places. While visiting my sister, and observing other patients, I noticed a lot of people did not have visitors or family checking in on them or spending time with them. I thought to myself, how could people just place someone away, and not check in on them. It baffled me to the point that it made me sad for them.

Well, 2008 had come and it was time for her to be released from the nursing facility. By that time she was able to do a little more for herself, but in reality, someone still needed to be with her during the day.

It was like I was beginning a new chapter in my life, such as being a mom to two people, one to my son of course and the other to my sister. She still had to go for doctor's appointments, physical therapy, occupational therapy, as well as speech therapy. She had to continue those appointments until things started to improve. She still needed assistance with bathing, getting dressed as well as meals being cooked for her daily.

Although I worked a full-time job, I still had to make sure those things were done for her. As I look back, I think about all of what I had to do and still do for her. I realize more and more it was the Lord's strength living on the inside that helped me.

Today she is doing much better, praise God! Although, she still lives with me and I still take care of her, she is getting around much better, she is better able to take care of her personal hygiene, and she is able to dress herself for the most part. She is very positive and because of her faith in God, she is able to stand and believe for the manifestation of her healing!

This by no means sums up everything I had to endure as a Caregiver. But it gives you some idea of what it was like for me. I never thought in a million years that I would be a Caregiver. It is not something anyone plans on being or grows up thinking they will become one day.

It is an unfortunate thing that happened to my sister, and I cannot change the past. But I can do everything I can to make her present and future better. I am very thankful that I am still able to assist her in becoming better daily.

Life is funny sometimes. We never know where it may take us specifically or what may happen that will change it. But one thing I know for sure is that when someone needs you and you accept the responsibility to help them, then make sure that you are prepared to give them your all. It is a lot of hard work and a lot of commitment. But I looked at it as if I would have been in my sister's shoes, she would have done the same thing for me.

Being a Caregiver is becoming more and more

common nowadays. But being a great Caregiver consists of putting the person's needs above your own in a lot of situations.

Remember, you are a Caregiver because someone needs you and because they cannot take care of themselves properly. Please know that what you do for them, God will do for you. His reward is the best reward you can ever imagine to receive. You truly are special!

Chapter 2

Take Care of You

If you do not remember anything else from this book, please remember this….take care of yourself! Taking care of another person can be draining emotionally, mentally, physically and financially. I do not know how many times I have seen so many Caregivers not take care of themselves. They are too busy taking care of the person they are looking after, by tending to their needs and they forget about themselves. You have to find ways to do take care of yourself. It may be going to the movies, reading a book, going shopping, or getting a massage. It may also be taking a vacation, whether for just a weekend or an extended one. You may even take the time to sit in a tub of water for relaxation. Those are just a few to name.

You have to take care of your body, mind and spirit. Finding time for you will only refresh you. It is not fair to you or the person that you are giving care to, if you do not take care of yourself. Too often we get caught up in doing things without considering ourselves. If you do not take care of you, frustration will come. For example, I found myself getting more frustrated when I had to do something for my sister, whether it was continuously taking her to her doctor's appointment, such as the neurologist, occupational therapist and physical therapist. I also had to setup her appointments as well as to make sure that they worked with my schedule and with other family members who assisted her.

I would prepare meals every day, sometimes both breakfast and dinner and help her with getting dressed, because she was unable to do it on her own. I also prepared her clothing for the week, which included washing and ironing and still had to do the cleaning of the house. I found myself not wanting to go on taking care of her and then I realized I was not taking care of me.

You see, I would feel guilty if I did not take her everywhere I went. And then I wound up letting it get the best of me. My sister never made me feel like I had to take her everywhere I went, but it was more of my feelings that caused me to think that way. I thought that I had to make sure she was still able to go places and do things that I did, since she did not ask for this horrible disease to come about in her life.

But I had to realized that it was not my fault either and I couldn't make it up to her by trying to make sure she always had something to do, even if it meant tiring myself out. I'm not saying that you should be completely selfish, but what I am saying is that you have to take time out for you. Even if it is only one day a week of nothing but me time, you have to do it. I will talk more about guilt and frustration in the latter chapter.

Now I know there may be some extreme cases, where you cannot get away for a long length of time, but even a short length of time will be worth every minute of it. You can ask your relatives to assist you. If you do not have any relatives who you can ask, check with your state for care giving assistance.

Women, by nature are nurturers. It is in our nature to take care of everyone else and to make sure that everyone has what they need. But we have to take care of ourselves as well. I cannot stress that enough. I see so many women who have given so much of themselves that they have nothing left to give to themselves or anyone else.

And the next thing you know they are taking their frustrations out on others. They look and feel worn out. Their hair and their skin are not properly taken care of. They become overweight or underweight from not eating healthy or not eating proper foods. They are not exercising in order to stay physically fit. And in order to physically take care of someone else, you have to be in good physical shape.

Caregivers tend to not have any confidence in or about themselves, because of all the effort that goes into the person who they are caring for. They have emotions that make them feel that all they were meant to do is to take care of others. And then they allow their dreams and their desires to disappear. Please do not allow that to happen to you. But if you have, then get the old you back with a new attitude.

Seek spiritual and/or professional counseling, if you need too. You are somebody and you deserve to have a life of your own. What were some things that you liked to do before you became a Caregiver? What made you feel good when you completed it? What is your passion? What are your strengths? Make a list of things, whether it is music, sports, traveling, gardening, shopping, painting, writing, decorating homes, shopping or visiting the less fortunate. There is something that you can do to separate you from being a Caregiver.

For me, one of the things that I enjoy is going to the gym. It relaxes me in a sense. Lifting weights, using the machines and even jogging made me feel really good. It refreshes me and I am able to take care of my body at the same time.

I also enjoy shopping and not necessarily spending money every time I go. I can enjoy just window shopping by seeing what the latest trend is. When it comes to window shopping for my home, I am able to see what I can do differently, whether it is changing the colors in the rooms or bedding. It gives me an opportunity to do something else. It doesn't matter if you are a man or a woman. You have to take care of yourself.

I know that there are numerous spouses taking care of their spouse as well as sons and daughters taking care of their elderly parents. And of course siblings taking care of disabled siblings. And I applaud you for what you are doing. For me personally, what keeps me going is the strength of God that I have within me. I realized that I had to be strong not only physically, but mentally and spiritually. And that is what has kept me all these years, even when I felt like giving up, giving out and giving in.

On purpose find something you like to do, and begin doing it. It is not going to happen on its own. You have to do something in order to see the results. And you have to start now! Time is going by pretty fast, if you haven't noticed. And if you keep putting it off, you will not accomplish those self-tasks that you know need to be completed. Remember that there is only one you, and if you do not keep your body and your spirit man strong, you will not last.

I cannot express how important it is and how it should be a priority in your life to take care of yourself. In order to

be the Caregiver you need to be, you will have to take care of

you! The time is NOW! Let's go!!

QUESTIONS FOR THOUGHT

What in this chapter really hit home for you?

_____

_____

_____

_____

_____

_____

What are some things you are doing to take care of YOURSELF?

_____

_____

_____

_____

_____

_____

_____

What are some things you are not doing that you want or need to do for YOURSELF?

_____

_____

_____

_____

_____

_____

_____

How do you feel when you're not doing things for YOURSELF?

Tired, drained, overwhelmed….

_____

_____

_____

_____

_____

_____

_____

List a few things YOU would like to start doing? Then give

YOURSELF a goal/deadline to start on those things.

_____

_____

_____

_____

_____

_____

_____

_____

_____

_____

_____

_____

_____

_____

_____

_____

_____

_____

NOTES/JOURNAL

_____

_____

_____

_____

_____

_____

_____

_____

_____

_____

_____

_____

_____

_____

_____

_____

_____

_____

_____

Chapter 3

Supportive Relationships

Regardless of whom you are or what you are experiencing, relationships are very important. I do not mean just any and every kind of relationship. I am talking about those relationships that can add to your life. I value the relationships that I have in my life. I make it a habit to be an asset to people and not a liability.

When you are a Caregiver, you will realize how important and how vital right relationships are. For the past eight years or so of my life, since I have been a Caregiver, I have been very fortunate to have different types of relationships in my life. It helped me to keep my sanity. I have people who will encourage me when I feel like giving up and I have people who will step up and assist me with my sister. I also have those who I can just talk to about how I am feeling when it comes to being a Caregiver. Even though they may not be a Caregiver, they are there to listen to me, which is very important.

Relationships are very important because it is a way of staying connected to others. I do believe that there are many different types of relationships for numerous reasons. I have some relationships where it is strictly for conversations about everyday life. Then I have some relationships where we just encourage one another. And then I have special relationships with a few people where I can go to and talk to about anything. Now that is only a few people. That is the type of relationship that requires a lot of trust.

I often see people that are afraid to have relationship with others because of past hurts because they did not want to make the time or they did not feel the necessity of it. I say that to say, do not allow that to continue to be your thinking. I know how it feels to be hurt by people and to have people walk out of my life when I needed them the most. I also know how it feels to have people help me take care of my sister and then decide to leave. And I did not want to deal with people after that. I felt like I had become so close to a few people and then once they hurt me, I thought to myself no more. But what I did not realize was that I would be missing out on new opportunities to meet new people. Whether we realize or not, or want to admit it, we need people in our lives.

Having relationships with the right people is very important and can add to your life. When I say the right people, I mean positive people who will uplift you, who will encourage you, and who will always have your best interest at heart. You are already dealing with enough in your life, by being a Caregiver. And the last thing you need to deal with is someone who is negative. In other words, someone who is always thinking the worst in every situation. They are constantly speaking negative things in your presence.

For example when I was going through the early stages of my sister being diagnosed with an autoimmune disease, we would often hear people say, "She will always be like that." or "She's not going to get better." Even the doctors would say there is nothing else that they could do. Now I expected the doctors to give their medical opinion. I just did not need to hear others to give their personal one, especially when it was negative. I was not trying to deny what she was diagnosed with. But I was not going to let it get the best of me or the best of her. I had to protect what she was hearing. It was important to have the right people, not only in her life, but in mine as well.

There are even family members who are not on the same page as you. They are negative and they make meaningless comments. They look at how you are now and not what you will become. They do not spiritually see the way you see. So they doubt what you vision for yourself. You will have to distance yourself from them. I had to do that exact same thing. I love all of my family members, but I had to make the decision to keep our environment and our surroundings positive. If the relationship, regardless if it was family, was not beneficial to me or to my sister in a positive way, then I distanced myself from them. Now that did not mean I wrote them off completely or did not love them. I still loved them, and still talked to them from time to time. But I would not allow them to be in my daily circle, so to speak. It was and still is important to me to keep my surroundings and my sister's surroundings positive as much as possible.

If you are constantly around someone who is always talking negative, doubt and unbelief or someone who always reminds you of what happened to someone they knew who had the same illness the person you are caring for had, let them go in the most loving way! It will hurt for a moment, but it will pay off later when you have peace in the situation. Trust me when I say, you will only do yourself well, when you eliminate negativity.

Accountability is great to have in special relationships. If there is something that I need help with, then I have learned to select the right people for every situation. If you need someone to be accountable to make sure you have taken time out for yourself monthly, then ask someone. Or if you need someone to just listen to you, then ask. It is ok to ask for help! We all need help some time in our lives. But we have to make sure that we ask the right people. Being surrounded by the right people can make a HUGE difference in your life. So choose wisely!

QUESTIONS FOR THOUGHT

What type of relationships do you have in your life?

_____

_____

_____

_____

_____

_____

Are they beneficial to your caregiving status?

_____

_____

_____

_____

_____

_____

Are there people around whom you consider negative? And what steps do you feel you need to take to distance yourself from the negativity?

_____

_____

_____

_____

_____

_____

Do you have any positive supporters in your life? If not, why….

_____

_____

_____

_____

_____

_____

NOTES/JOURNAL

Chapter 4

Remember Who You Are Taking Care Of

It does not matter whom you are taking care of. Remember, they are a person and they have their own identity. Sometimes when we have taken care of someone for a long time, we tend to forget that they are somebody and that they are an adult. They have their own opinions and they want their independence back as well.

We also forget that they were on their own at one time. They were making their own decisions, as well as paying their own bills and taking care of their own home such as cleaning and cooking without anyone's assistance in addition to scheduling their annual doctor's appointments when needed as well as driving themselves to those appointments. And now that we have to do that, we feel like we do not need to ask them for their opinions or ask them how they feel. I began to treat my sister that way a few years ago.

I started getting used to making all the decisions,

solely. A lot of times I did not even think to ask her what she thought or if she agreed. In 2007, her symptoms began to increase and her body began to decrease. So a lot of times she had no idea of what was going on.

When the doctor would tell me what I should do in many different situations, such as what type of medications they wanted to put her on or where they would suggest that I take her to certain places for a particular therapy, I would just make the best decision after prayer, and hardly ever asked my sister what she thought. She really was not aware of what was taking place, because of the attacks of the disease.

Well, after making those decisions, and my sister not being aware at the time, I had become so used to making all the decisions. Finally, a couple of years later, she started becoming more aware of things. She did not remember a lot of what had taken place but later I was able to explain to her what the doctor's wanted to do, so forth and so on.

But there became a point and time when my sister let me know that she wanted to be a part of the decision making.

And I agreed with her. She wanted to be treated like my sister and not her Caregiver. That was a challenge for me. But I had to make the adjustments. I put myself in her shoes and wondered how I would feel if it was the other way around. Would I want someone to make decisions without consulting me? For example, what I should wear, what I should eat, what bills should be paid and how much should be paid?

You see, even when it came to finances, I had to make decisions regarding that as well. When her monthly check would come in, I had to decide where and how to distribute the money to make sure that all the money was accounted for. I also had to make sure her savings account was being kept up as well. When medical bills would come in, I had to make sure that they were paid at all times. My sister really did not understand all that was going on.

Even when I would explain to her what was taking place as far as her finances, she only understood for the moment at that time. Does any of this sound familiar to you? Do you see yourself in my shoes? If so, then that is why I can say I understand what you are experiencing.

It may be a different level of Caregiving, but the point is, we have to remember who we are taking care of and we have to know that they are a person. They are the same person they were before we began taking care of them. It is just now they have some disabilities they are dealing with. And we are their voice, their hands and their feet at the moment.

I have been around other caregivers, whether in the doctor's office or in a department store. And I noticed how they speak to the person they are caring for. I have seen daughters talk to their mothers as if they were children. I have also seen sons treat their fathers like a stranger. It is amazing to me when the roles change, people can be very inconsiderate and very cold-hearted. I believe some people do not realize they are acting that way. It has become a part of them to the point, where it is just robotic motions. When a person has been taking care of someone for an especially long period of time, they tend to forget who they are caring for.

Take a moment alone and ask yourself, have you done

this a time or two? Have you made decisions for someone for so long, that you do not even think to ask for their input or value their opinion any more like you use to?

Do not just assume that your way is the best way without involving the person who you are caring for. If so, admit it, and then apologize for doing it. You can start all over again as long as you are breathing. We all have missed it numerous times in our lives. And that is alright as long as we recognized the mistakes, admit them and then learn from them.

No one is perfect at being a Caregiver. It is an everyday and ongoing process. And as long as we realize that we made a mistake as well as do our best to correct it, then everything will turn out alright. The person that you are caring for will appreciate the fact that you admit your mistakes in regards to not treating them like they are an adult. And they will respect you for it as well as value the relationship even more. Everyone wants to be treated with respect, whether they are disabled or not! And we owe that to the person we are caring for.

Remember, they did not ask for these life changing events that have taken place. They did not know that what has taken place, would stop them from living the life they were living before you became their Caregiver. But now that they are in that particular place in life, they need to feel like they are a whole human being. They also need to feel like they are contributing to the decisions that are being made for them and not merely depending on someone else decisions. Remember they are somebody!

QUESTIONS FOR THOUGHT

Does any part of this chapter relate to you?

_____

_____

_____

_____

_____

_____

How do you treat the person that you are taking care of? Be

honest....

_____

_____

_____

_____

_____

_____

Do you forget sometimes that you are taking care of someone that can think for themselves?

_____

_____

_____

_____

_____

_____

Have you forgiven yourself when you did not treat the person the way they should have been treated?

_____

_____

_____

_____

_____

_____ -

_____

UPLIFTING AND ENCOURAGING CAREGIVERS

Have you apologized to the person you're caring for when you did not treat them right? If so, how did it make you feel? If not, then just simply say "I'm sorry".

_____

_____

_____

_____

_____

_____

Are you learning to be patient? If so, in what way?

_____

_____

_____

_____

_____

_____

_____

NOTES/JOURNAL

JOHNNITA ROBINSON

Chapter 5

Get Rid of Guilt and Frustration

When you think of either word, you tend to think of the other. Frustration can come into play when guilt tries to take you over. It is a negative feeling that begins to play with your emotions as it starts in your mind. When you begin to make plans to do something for yourself, the thought comes, "Why should I go anywhere?" The person I am caring for cannot go. Or why should I be able to attend conferences, go to musical plays, out to dinner or even go shopping? I know for me, I would feel guilty if I had decided to do things that did not include my sister, although she never made me feel that way. But in the beginning of taking care of her, I felt a huge amount of guilt.

For the first few years of her diagnosis, I would hardly go anywhere, even if it was just to the movies, to dinner, a date or even vacations. I would often feel guilty, if I even thought about going anywhere without her.

When I would wake up to get my day started by

getting dressed and going to work, my mind would always go back to how she must be feeling or to what is she thinking now that she is unemployed and I am still able to work.

I would replay it in my mind all day, the thought of her not being able to do what she had done all her life, and that was whatever she wanted to do.

I was feeling guilty because she was not able to go and enjoy the activities or functions that were taking place. So, if she could not then why should I. Even though it was not my fault nor hers, I felt I had no right to have fun or enjoy myself. Just knowing that my sister could not attend, made me feel horrible on the inside. This went on for a while, until I realized that I could not continue to go on like this. I had to keep reminding myself that this situation was not my fault!

Does any of this sounds familiar? Have you attempted to do some things for yourself, but felt guilty about it? Did you allow frustration to set in because of the guilt?

Have you ever decided not to participate or not go

somewhere because of feeling like you are doing something wrong without the person you are caring for? That is guilt! Do you get frustrated because you said no to numerous offers, because of the person you were caring for could not participate?

If so, you cannot allow yourself to feel that way. But if you do, then you need to re-channel your thinking. You are not to blame for what happened to the person you are caring for. You have to take the time to enjoy yourself, during the process of being a Caregiver.

Guilt comes from being responsible or blameworthy of something. Being a Caregiver that needs and wants to take care of themselves by enjoying the things that make them happy, should not include guilt or frustration.

You should not allow yourself to feel guilty by wanting to take a vacation. You need that time to become refreshed. Do not listen to guilty thoughts when they try to overtake you. Let those thoughts know that they do not have the right to resonate in you. All those thoughts will only lead to frustration. You have no reason to feel guilty! These feelings and thoughts can cause sickness, stress and numerous other things to overcome your mental and emotional state. It can also cause lack of confidence in what you are doing and who you are. It is not worth it. I repeat it is not worth it. But you are worth it!

You are worth more than allowing yourself to feel guilty or to feel frustration. If you continue to allow guilt and frustration be a part of your life, you will never be able to move forward and you will never be able to have the peace you need in order to be better. Do not allow guilt to set in! You have nothing to feel guilty about!

I have seen what guilt and frustration can do to people that allow it to overtake them. It not only affects you mentally and spiritually, but it can affect you physically. But even more importantly, it can affect your health. Think about it. Your body was not meant to carry things that could affect you negatively.

Let's put it another way. When you think on things that are not positive, how does it make you feel? When you allow yourself to carry things that weigh you down, how does it make your feel? It begins to make you feel out of control. It makes you feel like it is too much to bear and it makes you feel like you are paralyzed and cannot move anywhere physically. Well, that is exactly what guilt and frustration can do to you, if you allow it too.

Guilt is something you receive when you have done wrong. In the case of being a Caregiver you have done nothing wrong. So do not allow yourself to succumb to guilt! Do not allow guilty thoughts to keep replaying in your mind every time you decide to do something for you. When you look at the person you are caring for, realize that you are doing the best that you know how to do and know that you are giving that person the best care that you know how to give. But also know that if you mess up, it is okay. Get back up and start all over again. That is the great thing about life. As long as you are alive, you can always start over.

Remember, no more guilt, no more frustration! You have what it takes to refuse to allow yourself to be overcome with either. You are stronger than what you think. You can

do this!

QUESTIONS FOR THOUGHT

Have you ever experienced any guilt and frustration?

_____

_____

_____

_____

_____

How do you respond or react to the guilt and frustration you feel?

_____

_____

_____

_____

_____

_____

_____

_____

Why do you feel guilt and frustration?

_____

_____

_____

_____

_____

_____

_____

After reading this chapter, do you now understand it is not your fault for what has happened to the person you are caring for and why?

_____

_____

_____

_____

_____

_____

_____

_____

NOTES/JOURNAL

_____

_____

_____

_____

_____

_____

_____

_____

_____

_____

_____

_____

_____

_____

_____

_____

_____

_____

_____

_____

Chapter 6

Moving Forward

I am sure a lot has happened in your life while being a Caregiver, whether the person you caring for has either become better or possibly a little worse. Maybe you did not make the best decisions while taking care of that person. You may feel like the person you are caring for should have received more help sooner or you may feel that you should have taken them to better doctors, such as well-known specialists.

You may even feel like you should have listened more to the person you were caring for by asking them about their simple needs or desires such as the type of clothing that makes them feel comfortable or what types of food do they want that would be healthier for them. Or even where they would like to go for vacation, what their likes and dislikes are about their living situation or what can you do to make their life easier. Maybe you should have kept them more informed of their savings and checking accounts.

Whatever it is, remember that all of that took place up until you read this book. And whatever has taken place, it is now in the past. There is nothing you can do about the past. But you sure can change the present and the future.

Do not allow anyone to make you feel like the decisions you have made up until now have been inexcusable. Things have happened in all of our lives and sometimes we just did not know how to make the best decisions.

I realize it is so easy for people to say what you should have and should not have done, when they are not in the same position that you are in. And for those people who thought I did not make the best decisions or who felt like I should have made another choice I would tell them to try being in my position and see what they would do.

I had to make some decisions over the years for my sister that was based on what the doctors suggested which was fine because that is what good doctors are for. But there were some decisions I had to really pray about. I had to seek God for His direction as to what was best for my sister, even if it went against what others may have suggested.

I can remember some of the decisions I made were not

received by others in my family, and I would second guess myself quite a bit. The decision to have her placed in a nursing home was not popular, but that was the best decision I could make at that time, and actually it wound up being a good decision, not only for her, but for me as well.

It is not easy trying to direct someone else's life, let alone make medical decisions for them, especially when you have your own life to direct. But I will tell you this. I did not allow myself to walk around very long with guilt from some of the decisions that may not have been the best. I did the best I could with what knowledge I had.

So I applaud you for what you have done to help the person you are caring for. But it is time to move forward and leave the past in the past. If you keep focusing on what you could have done differently in the past, you will never be able to move forward to a better future.

Life is too short to keep focusing on what should have or could have done. I truly believe what you think on can consume you either in a negative way or in a positive way. That is why it is important to think on and to focus on the good in life, but more importantly to focus on God's Word. It

is vital for you to know that the past is behind you and that a great future is ahead of you, as long as you do not allow the past to rob you of your future!

QUESTIONS FOR THOUGHT

Do you find it hard to move forward? If so, why?

_____

_____

_____

_____

_____

_____

_____

Write down the things you know that need to be left in the past.

_____

_____

_____

_____

_____

_____

_____

_____

After reading this chapter, do you understand why it is best to move forward?

_____

_____

_____

_____

_____

_____

_____

Now, have you decided to move forward?

_____

_____

_____

_____

_____

_____

_____

NOTES/JOURNAL

_____

_____

_____

_____

_____

_____

_____

_____

_____

_____

_____

_____

_____

_____

_____

_____

_____

_____

JOHNNITA ROBINSON

Chapter 7

Never Give Up

No matter what you have gone through, or what you are going through, do not ever give up. Do not ever think it will not get better. Trust me, I understand what it feels like to want to just say, "I am done with this", "I can not take care of anyone else", "It is too much to deal with", "There's just too many doctor's appointments that she needs to attend", "Who am I going to get to help me with these appointments?" or "Who can I leave her with, while I go away for the weekend?"

I know what it is like to come home and the house is in shambles, food is on the floor from where my sister was eating and was not able to clean it up or there are holes in the wall from where the wheelchair accidentally ran into it. Or maybe my sister did not have such a good day due to her symptoms or I had to be her encourager.

Sometimes you may feel like you are alone. I too, understand how it feels to make so many decisions alone. Although you may not be completely alone, you just may feel that way.

There were many nights I would just cry and wonder what is going on. Why did this happen to my sister? How could we have prevented these things from happening? Or how come this happened to me? Why do I have to be a caregiver? And I should be living my life totally free of taking care of anyone, especially since my son is an adult.

There were days and nights I wanted to just walk away and never look back. But deep down, I knew I could not pursue those thoughts. If I had given up, then no telling where my sister would be at this moment. She needed me more than anything to help her get to where she is today.

You probably have felt the same way or still feel that way. But I can assure you, it will get better as long as you decide not to give up, you will get through your circumstances.

You may think there is no way to make time for yourself. You have tried and tried, but you cannot seem to make the necessary adjustments or it seems like every time you make time for yourself, something happens to where you are always needed. I have been there numerous times.

No matter what happens, you cannot give up. If you give up now, then you will never know what you could have accomplished. It will be challenging trying to balance your schedule as well as the other person's schedule you are caring for. It will also be challenging to make sure their needs are met in addition to your own. But it is not impossible! It can be done. You just have to make the time to do it. You have to discipline yourself enough to make it happen.

I have been around a number of people over the years who have given up in life because of their circumstances, and I must say without faith they are lost. They have allowed their challenges to overtake them and caused them to be weak and in fear. Do not allow that to happen to you.

As I stated earlier in the book, it was God's help that kept me rooted and kept me stable to accomplish what I needed to do. I would seek His guidance and His direction on how to find the balance in my life.

It was not an overnight change. It was a daily process. The more I did it, the easier it became. So that is why I am telling you, not to give up! You have not come this far too just give in. You can do this! Trust God and trust yourself. If you are not sure of how to balance everything, then ask someone. There are too many people in this world that have the solution to your problem. You just have to speak up and ask. If you do not, then no one will ever know you need help. Got it?!

Remember that you are not the first person to go through what you are going through and you will not be the last one. Everyone has gone through something in life. But what separates you from those who did not achieve what they needed to are those who gave up. You are not a quitter! You are a winner!

QUESTIONS FOR THOUGHT

Have you ever felt like giving up?

_____

_____

_____

_____

_____

Do you understand the importance of not giving up?

_____

_____

_____

_____

Will you make the decision not to give up no matter?

_____

_____

_____

_____

_____

NOTES/JOURNAL

JOHNNITA ROBINSON

<u>CONCLUSION</u>

Being a Caregiver myself, I know what it takes to get the job done. I know the selfless acts that are needed to make sure that the needs are met for the person that is being cared for. But just as importantly, as a Caregiver, you have to make sure your needs are met as well. You have to make sure that you are taking the necessary steps to be uplifted, refreshed and refueled.

You have to make sure that you make time for activities you desire to do and make sure that you are taking time out for you. If it is nothing but going to the movies, going out to dinner weekly or even biweekly, playing sports, joining a gym, taking on a new hobby such as painting, interior decorating or whatever you feel you need to do to be better, you have to do it!

Do not let another year or even another six months go by without making the necessary adjustments. Remember, if you don't, then you will not only be good for the person you are caring for, but you will not be good for yourself. Please, please, please hear me when I say this. You must take your life back as much as you can to do the things that will please you!

Also, do not allow yourself to feel guilt any longer, if you are doing that. You did the best that you could with what you knew and with what you had. It is time to move forward to brighter days which are ahead. I firmly believe that for you. It has happened for me as well as the person I am caring for. We made a decision together to stay positive as much as we could while in this situation. We have learned to lean on and trust God no matter what. When others left, God never did.

When I made the decision a long time ago that I was going to take better care of me, it changed my life in more ways than you can imagine. I not only finished college, but I took numerous vacations, as well as wrote this book, and it has made me better.

I have other projects that I am working on to not only make me better but to make those around me better as well. I am determined to uplift and to encourage as many Caregivers as I can.

I want Caregivers to know how much I empathize with them and how much I understand the challenges and the pain that comes with being a Caregiver. But I also want them to know that they can still have a bright future which can supersede the past.

Being a Caregiver with God's help, has contributed to my being

stronger, bolder and more courageous than I have ever thought I could be. I am at more peace now than I have ever been before and I am continuously living out the plan and purpose that God has for me. I am looking forward to what the future has for me!

JOHNNITA ROBINSON

SCRIPTURES TO STAND ON WHILE BEING A CAREGIVER

Anger- Ephesians 4:26- Be angry, and do not sin. Do not let the sun go down on your wrath.

Anxious- Philippians 4:6- Be anxious for nothing, but in everything by prayer and supplication, with thanksgiving let your requests be made known to God.

Boldness-Hebrews 13:6- So we may boldly say, The Lord is my helper, I will not fear. What can man do to me?

Confidence- 1 John 5:14- Now this is the confidence that we have in God, that if we ask anything according to His will, he hears us. And if we know that He hears us, whatever we ask, we know that we have what we asked of Him.

Fear- 2 Timothy 1:7- For God has not given us the spirit of fear, but of power, love and a sound mind.

Give- Luke 6:38- Give and it shall be given unto you, good measured, pressed down and shaken together, running over will be put into your bosom. For with the same measure that you use, it will be measured back to you.

Healing- 1 Peter 2:24- Who Himself bore our sins in His own body on the tree, that we having died to sins, might live for righteousness, by whose stripes you were healed. Isaiah 53:4, 5 Surely He has borne our griefs and carried our sorrows, yet we esteemed Him stricken, Smitten by God, and afflicted. But He was wounded for our transgressions. He was bruised for our iniquities; the chastisement for our peace was upon Him, and by His stripes we are healed.

Joy- Nehemiah 8:10- The Joy of the Lord is our strength

Love- 1 Corinthians 13:4-8- Love is patient, love is kind. It does not envy, it does not boast, it is not proud. It does not dishonor others, it is not self-seeking, it is not easily angered, and it keeps no record of wrongs. Love does not delight in evil but rejoices with the truth. It always protects, always trusts, always hopes, and always perseveres. Love never fails.

Never Alone- Hebrew 13:5 -Let your conduct be without covetousness, be content with such things as you have. For He Himself, has said I will never leave nor forsake you.

Patience- James 1:2- Consider it pure joy, my brothers and sisters, whenever you face trials of many kinds, because you know that the testing of your faith produces perseverance.

Purpose- Jeremiah 1:5 –Before I formed you in the womb I knew you, before you were born I set you apart. Jeremiah 29:11- For I know the plans I have for you, declares the Lord, plans to prosper you and not to harm, plans to give you hope and a future.

Peace-John 14:27- Peace I leave with you, my peace I give you. I do not give to you as the world gives. Do not let your hearts be troubled and do not be afraid.

Reward- Galatians 6:9- Let us not become weary in doing good, for at the proper time we will reap a harvest if we do not give up.

Trust- Proverbs 3:5-Trust in the Lord with all your heart and lean not on your understanding.

Wisdom- Colossians 1:9 -For this reason, since the day we heard about you, we have not stopped praying for you. We continually ask God to fill you with knowledge of his will through all the wisdom and understanding that the Spirit gives. Ephesians 1: 17 I keep asking that the God of our Lord Jesus Christ, the glorious Father, may give you the Spirit of wisdom and revelation, so that you may know him better.

JOHNNITA ROBINSON

<u>PRAYER</u>

LORD, I THANK YOU FOR HELPING ME TO BE THE BEST CAREGIVER I CAN BE. THANK YOU FOR STRENGTHING ME WHENEVER I NEED IT THE MOST. SURROUND ME WITH POSITIVE PEOPLE. SURROUND ME WITH THOSE WHO WILL UPLIFT AND ENCOURAGE ME. AND THOSE WHO WILL HAVE MY BACK. AS I HONOR THE PERSON I AM CARING FOR, I KNOW YOU WILL HONOR ME. HELP ME TO CONTINOUSLY GO ABOVE AND BEYOND AS A CAREGIVER. GIVE ME WISDOM IN EVERY AREA OF MY LIFE SO THAT I CAN BE A BETTER PERSON. HELP ME TO LEAVE THE PAST IN THE PAST, KNOWING I DID THE BEST THAT I COULD. LEAD ME INTO THIS GREAT FUTURE I HAVE BECAUSE OF YOUR DIRECTION.

.

JOHNNITA ROBINSON

CONTACT INFORMATION

Email: robinsonjohnnita@gmail.com **(Speaking Engagements)**

FB Page: www.facebook.com/uplifting&encouragingcaregivers

(Like and Comment on the FB Page as well as be encouraged)

JOHNNITA ROBINSON

www.ingramcontent.com/pod-product-compliance
Lightning Source LLC
Chambersburg PA
CBHW062012040426

42447CB00010B/2009